Quick Tips

for Faster Fingers

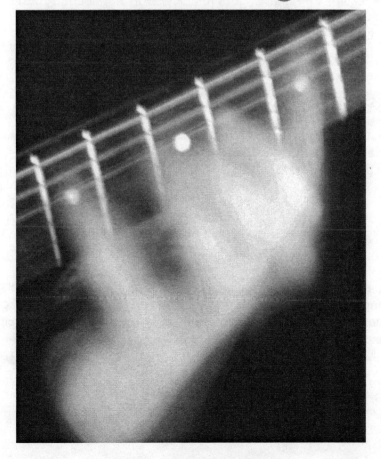

Don J. MacLean

Text editing by: Jeneane. McKenzie
Photography by: Michael Rafter (604) 910-5029

National Library of Canada Cataloguing in Publication Data

MacLean, Don J., 1968-
  Quick tips for faster fingers [music] / Don J. MacLean ; Jeneane McKenzie, editor.

ISBN 1-896595-10-3

  1. Guitar--Studies and exercises. I. McKenzie, Jeneane, 1968- II. Title.
MT585.M162 2003   787.87'193   C2002-911463-2

Quantity discounts are available on bulk purchases of this book for educational purposes. For information please contact Agogic Publishing 406-109 Tenth Street, New Westminster, British Columbia, V3M 3X7, (604) 290-2692.

Visit us on our website:
http://www.agogic.biz
for free downloads
and product information.

Contents

Chapter 1   Basics

Chapter 2   How to Practice

Chapter 3   Vibrato

Chapter 4   Alternate Picking

Chapter 5   Hammer-ons and Pull-offs

Chapter 6   Tapping

Chapter 7 Sweep Picking

About the Author

Don J. MacLean is an active freelance guitarist, composer and educator. His musical training includes studies at the Royal Conservatory of Music, Humber College, and York University, where he obtained his B.A. (Dbl. Hons. Maj.) in music and psychology. His twenty years of teaching, performing and composing have made Don a highly sought-after expert for workshops, seminars and master classes.

Don J. MacLean is the author of:

The World of Scales: A Compendium of Scales for the Modern Guitar Player
The World of Scales: A Compendium of Scales for all Instruments

Guitar Essentials: Chord Master
Guitar Essentials: Chord Master Expanded Edition
Guitar Essentials: Scale Master 1
Guitar Essentials: Improviser
Guitar Essentials: Chord and Scale Master Series

Music Essentials: Improviser

Absolute Essentials of Music Theory

Fit Fingers Book 1
Fit Fingers Book 2

Quick Tips for Faster Fingers
Quick Tips: Basic Chords for Guitar
Quick Tips: Basic Scales for Guitar

Mega Chops: Mozart for Pick-Style Guitar
Mega Chops: Bach for Pick-Style Guitar
Mega Chops: Corelli for Pick-Style Guitar
Mega Chops: Vivaldi for Pick-Style Guitar

Introduction

Welcome to Quick Tips for Faster Fingers. This book contains 54 pieces and exercises chosen to improve the technique of the beginner to intermediate player.

One of the most frequent questions I am asked by my students is: "How can I improve my technique?" The answer to this question is: practice, practice, practice. The more time you spend on the guitar, the better you will get. What you practice and how you practice, determines your level of accomplishment. One of the best ways to improve your technique is to play music written for other instruments. An extra benefit to this, is that you will encounter melody lines not otherwise found in the guitar literature.

The examples that appear in this book are excerpts from Fit Fingers Books 1&2, which will provide you with further techniques, studies and pieces.

Chapter 1

Basics

Guitar Anatomy

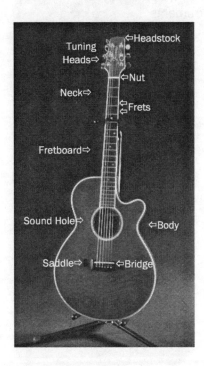

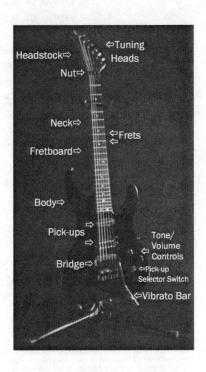

How to Hold the Guitar

The best way for a right-handed player to hold the guitar, is to position the guitar on the left leg. The right leg should be used for the left-handed guitarist. This may feel uncomfortable at first, but positioning the guitar on the appropriate leg will make it easier for you to stretch your fingers.

OK

Best

How to Hold a Pick

Guitar picks or plectrums, come in a wide variety of shapes and sizes. It is best to use either a medium or heavy pick. Thin picks flop around too much and will slow you down. The pick should be held between the thumb and the first finger as shown below.

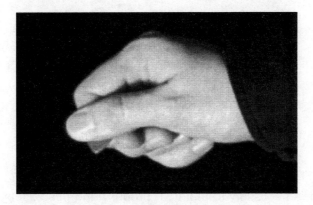

When you play the guitar you will either pick an individual string or strum several simultaneously. You should use only the very tip of the pick to strike the string.

String

Front View.

View from Bottom.

Top-down View.

In order to lessen the confusion between left and right-handed guitar players, the term fret-hand will be used to denote the actual hand you use to play any notes on the neck of the guitar. Your fret-hand fingers are numbered accordingly:

The thumb is generally not used to play notes.

Fret-hand Position

To produce clear notes it is necessary to maintain proper hand positioning. The palm of your hand should not make contact with the neck of the guitar—use only the tips of your fret-hand fingers. Position the fingers as close as possible to the metal fret wire. Placing your finger on top of the fret wire will produce a muffled note. Your thumb should be placed on the back of the neck in line with your second or third finger. When your hand is in proper position, a thick highlighter will fit between your palm and the neck of the guitar.

Front View.

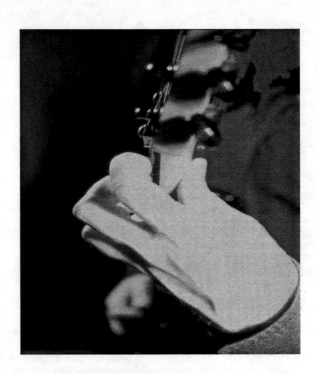

Side View.

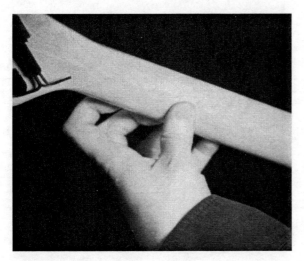

Rear View.

View from Bottom. Note that there is enough space to fit a highlighter between the palm and the neck.

Music Notation

Guitar music can be notated in four different ways: standard notation, tablature, rhythm/slash notation and neck diagrams or grids. This book uses only standard notation and tablature.

Standard Notation

Standard notation indicates the pitch of a note and also its duration. In standard notation the first symbol you will encounter is called a clef. A clef is a symbol used to indicate the pitch of a particular line. Guitar music is written in the treble clef. The **treble clef** is sometimes called the "G" clef because it indicates the position of the note G. The musical alphabet consists of the first seven letters of the alphabet: A—B—C—D—E—F—G. An easy way to remember the notes in the treble clef is to use the following mnemonics:

Every Good Boy Deserves Fudge (notes on lines)

Treble
Clef
↓

FACE (notes in spaces)

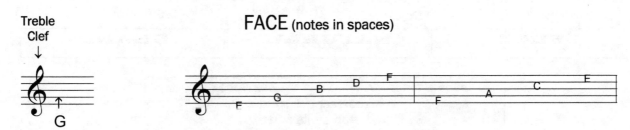

A Quick Overview of Tablature

In tablature, each horizontal line represents a string. The strings are numbered from the thinnest (1) to the thickest (6). The numbers on these lines represent the frets that you need to place your fingers on.

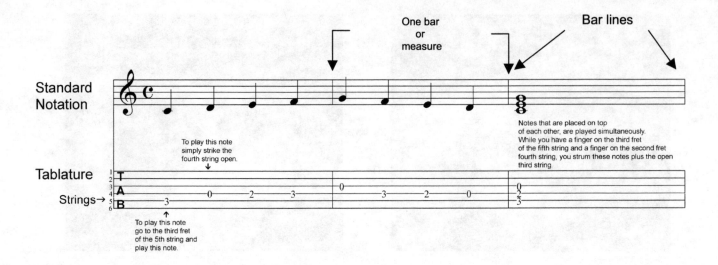

One bar or measure

Bar lines

Standard Notation

Tablature

Strings→

To play this note simply strike the fourth string open.

To play this note go to the third fret of the 5th string and play this note.

Notes that are placed on top of each other, are played simultaneously. While you have a finger on the third fret of the fifth string and a finger on the second fret fourth string, you strum these notes plus the open third string.

The Fretboard

UNDERSTANDING SHARPS (♯) AND FLATS (♭)

The names of the notes used in music come from the first seven letters of the alphabet: A–B–C–D–E–F–G. The distance of one fret is called a **semitone** or a **half step**. A **whole tone** or **tone** is the distance of two frets.

- If you raise a **natural note** (♮) by one semitone, the note will become a sharp. A natural note is a note that is not sharp or flat.
- If you lower a natural note one semitone, it will become a flat.
- By raising a flat (♭), one semitone, you obtain a natural note.
- Lowering a sharp (♯) one semitone, will give you a natural note.

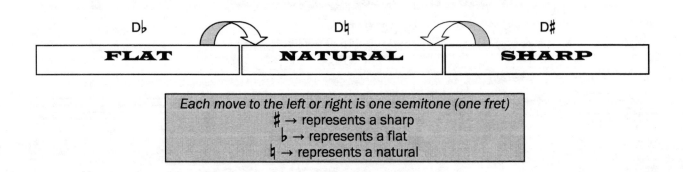

Each move to the left or right is one semitone (one fret)
♯ → represents a sharp
♭ → represents a flat
♮ → represents a natural

For example:
- If you raise an F one fret, it becomes an F♯.
- If you raise a D♭ one fret, it becomes a D♮.
- If you lower a G one fret, it becomes a G♭.
- If you lower a G♯ one fret, it becomes a G♮.

Enharmonic Equivalents

Enharmonic equivalents are notes that sound the same but are written with different letter-names. For example, the F♯ and G♭ are both found on the 2nd fret of the sixth string and sound identical. G♯ and A♭ both share the 1st fret of the third string. Context determines whether a note should be called an F♯ or a G♭. Here are a few other notes you should know about:

B♯ = C   E♯ = F   F♭ = E   C♭ = B

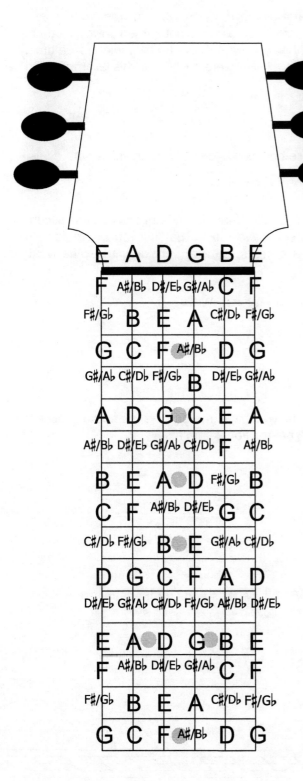

Tip 1: The grid on the left shows the letter-names of the notes on the guitar. The quickest way to learn these notes is to memorize the location of the natural notes. Once you know the location of the natural notes, you can very easily determine the location of any sharps or flats. Notice how E—F, and B—C are adjacent to one another (i.e., no frets between them), the rest of the natural notes have one fret between them.

Tip 2: The most efficient way to learn the fretboard is to take a string each week and memorize the location of the natural notes. The first 3 days of the week should be spent moving up and down the sixth string, naming the notes as you land on them. The next four days should be spent picking random notes on the neck and then identifying each note as quickly as possible. Repeat this procedure for the remaining strings.

Tip 3: The notes on the 12th fret have the same letter-names as the open strings. The notes above the 12th fret repeat, so once you learn the notes up to the 12th fret, you will already know the notes found on the remaining frets. You should also notice that the notes on the 6th and 1st strings have identical letter-names.

Rhythm

Levels of Rhythmic Activity

Music is usually organized in a repeatable accent pattern known as meter. In free time, music unfolds with an unpredictable accent pattern. If a performer plays a note, then several others quickly, then pauses for a while and plays additional notes, you would have an example of free time. This means that there is no time signature being used. If we were to notate this example with vertical slashes, here is what we would have:

       I   **IIIII**   **I II**

The vertical slashes represent the notes and the distance between each slash represents time.

Pulse/Beat

You will occasionally encounter music where each beat is an equal distance apart, but the accent pattern does not appear to repeat. In this instance you have music that has an unpredictable occurrence of strong and weak beats. Strong beats are beats that are very definite, while weak beats are of a more subtle nature.

     S   W   S   S   S   W   W   S   W

S = strong
W = weak

Meter

When you have a recurring repeatable accent pattern, you have meter. The repeatable accent pattern will consist of a combination of strong and weak beats. For example:

2/4 time consists of:
S   W

3/4 time consists of:
S   W   W

4/4 time consists of:
S   W   M   W   (M stands for medium weak)

5/4 time consists of:
S   W   S   W   W
or
S   W   W   S   W

S W M W   S   W   W   S W S W W *or:* S W W S W

Time Values

The most common time signature, 4/4, (pronounced four-four) is often abbreviated with a fancy "C" and called common time. In 4/4, the whole note receives four beats or counts. The half note receives two beats and the quarter note receives one beat. Eighth notes each receive half of a beat.

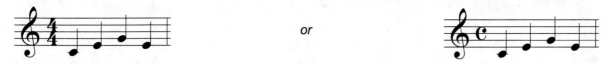

or

Note Durations

Note Durations

Eighth notes are sometimes written without connecting beams:

The whole note receives 4 beats; the half note receives 2 beats; a quarter note receives 1 beat and an eighth note receives 1/2 of a beat; a sixteenth note receives 1/4 of a beat and the triplet receives 1/3 of a beat.

Rest Durations

Rest Durations

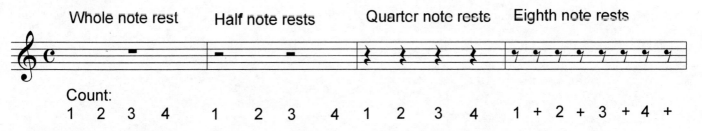

Time Signatures

A time signature is used to indicate the strong and weak beats in a measure and also which note value receives one beat. In **Simple Time** (2/2, 2/4, 2/8, 3/2, 3/4, 3/8, 4/2, 4/4, 4/8), the top number of the time signature indicates the number of beats per measure while the bottom number indicates the type of note that receives one beat. For example:

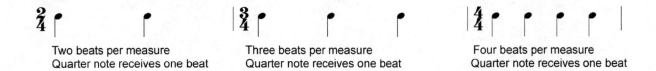

Two beats per measure
Quarter note receives one beat

Three beats per measure
Quarter note receives one beat

Four beats per measure
Quarter note receives one beat

In Simple time you tap your foot on each beat. In **Compound Time**, (6/4, 6/8, 6/16, 9/4, 9/8, 9/16, 12/4, 12/8, 12/16) you should tap your foot on each major beat division. In 6/8 time the measure is divided into two (1 2 3), (4 5 6). Nine-eight time has three main divisions (1 2 3), (4 5 6), (7 8 9). Twelve-eight time contains 4 main divisions (1 2 3), (4 5 6), (7 8 9), (10 11 12). In 6/8, you would count 1 2 3 4 5 6, but only tap your foot on 1 and 4. In 9/8, you would count 1 2 3 4 5 6 7 8 9, and tap your foot on 1, 4 and 7. In 12/8 time, you count 1 2 3 4 5 6 7 8 9 10 11 12, and tap your foot on 1, 4, 7 and 10.

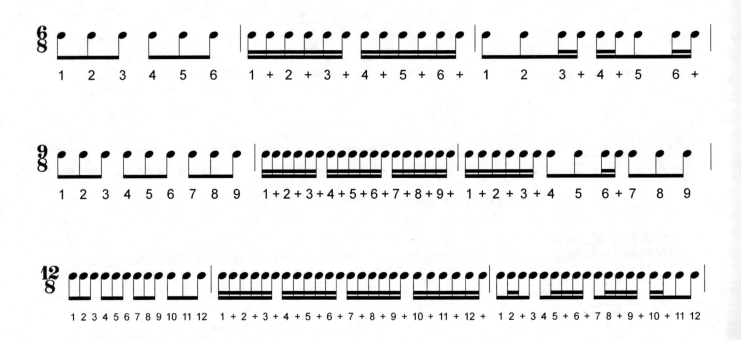

Dotted and Tied Notes

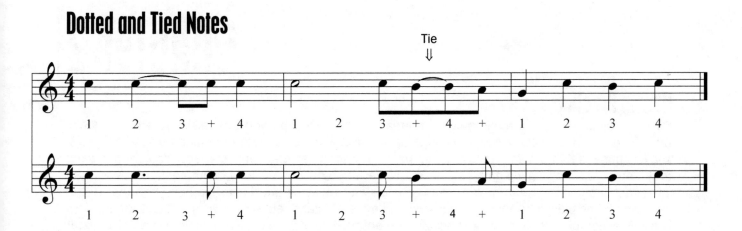

Ties and dots are used to increase the time value of the notes they follow. A dot increases the time value of a note by half. A half note receives 2 beats; a dotted half note receives 3 beats. A quarter note receives one beat; a dotted quarter note receives one and a half beats. An eighth note receives half of a beat; a dotted eighth note receives half of a beat plus one quarter of a beat (in other words 3/4's of a beat).

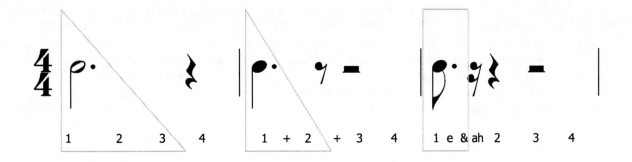

The notes in a tie are of the same pitch. A tie increases the time value of a note by the value of the second note. You do not pick the second note of the tie. You simply sustain the note for the duration of the first note plus the value of the note it is tied to.

Repeats

Instead of writing out the same music twice, repeats are used.

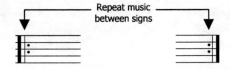

First and Second Endings

To perform first and second endings, the passage is repeated but the ending is different the second time.

Chapter 2

How to Practice

Consistency is one of the most important variables that will allow you to achieve your guitar goals. Our muscles and nervous system are able to adapt quickly to repeated demands placed on them. The key here, is that the demands must be made repeatedly for the body to adapt. You are not going to get stronger by lifting weights only once. To get strong you need to workout consistently with an intelligent program. The same is true for music—your muscles and fingertips have to adapt to the demands being placed on them so that new and more efficient neural pathways can be formed. This is easily accomplished by playing everyday with an intelligent program. You will progress at a faster rate if you practice thirty minutes each day as opposed to playing for an hour every other day.

Once you determine the amount of time you can practice each day, take that time and divide it in half. To increase your technical ability, the first half of your practice session should be spent performing exercises, scales, arpeggios, etc., and the second half devoted to application. By application, I am referring to the reason you originally picked up the instrument—to play songs. It is very important that you divide your time up this way. Let's say you have a half an hour a day that you can devote to playing the guitar. The first fifteen minutes should be spent on technique building exercises and the last fifteen minutes should be devoted to practicing and learning new songs. The reason you should do it this way, is because it is very easy to get lost in the songs and lose track of time. If you practice the songs first, you will usually find that your half hour is up and you didn't play a single technique exercise. Also, practicing your scales, chords and warm-up exercises first, will allow you to warm-up—making it easier to play the songs that follow. If more time materializes in the day, you can either repeat the cycle, or consider it free time and play whatever you want.

The pieces presented in this book can be included in the technique portion of your practice session or in your repertoire section. Either way, you will find that the pieces will make you a better player.

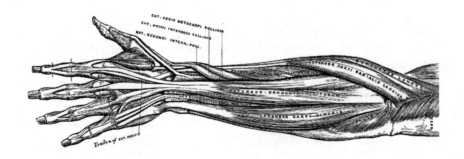

Chapter 3

Vibrato

To add variety and a bit of colour to notes, you will find vibrato to be an indispensable technique. In vibrato, you take a note and slightly pull it sharp and then return it to its original pitch. This process is repeated several times. Depending on the desired effect this can be done slowly or rapidly.

There are two main types of vibrato. The most common form used in rock, pop, folk, country and blues is performed by moving the fret-hand finger up and down in relation to the string. In essence, you are moving your finger perpendicular to the string. Some guitarists favour a subtle vibrato where the note is only moved slightly. Others prefer to employ a wide vibrato in which the string is moved aggressively up and down. A second type of vibrato that is used by classical guitarists is performed parallel to the string. To perform this type of vibrato you must fret the note in the middle of the fret and then rock your finger side-to-side along the length of the string.

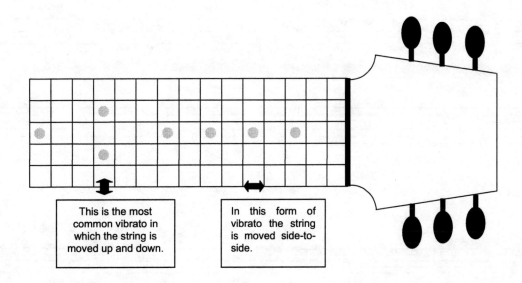

This is the most common vibrato in which the string is moved up and down.

In this form of vibrato the string is moved side-to-side.

Unless it is quite pronounced, vibrato is not symbolized at all in sheet music. The reason for this is that it is assumed that the guitarist will add vibrato where appropriate. Generally, you will find that vibrato will be used on most notes that have a duration of a quarter note or longer. Depending on the tempo of the song you may use vibrato on eighth and even sixteenth notes. When it is symbolized, vibrato is denoted as:

Vibrato Exercise # 1
Practice this exercise with both types of vibrato.

Jupiter
From The Planets Op. 32
Excerpt

G. Holst
Arr. by: Don J. MacLean

Pomp and Circumstance

E. Elgar
Arr. by: Don J. MacLean

Quick Tips for Faster Fingers

Swan Lake
Theme

P. Tchaikovsky
Arr. by Don J. MacLean

Chapter 4

Alternate Picking

Alternate picking is the most common and efficient way to play notes on individual strings. When you learn to play new songs, you can safely assume that alternate picking should be used. Alternate picking requires that you strike the first note with a down-stroke (⊓) and the next note with an up-stroke (v). The pattern is repeated for each successive note.

      Here is how to play the first alternate picking exercise shown below. To start the exercise, begin on the first string, 1st fret. The number combination 1-2-3-4, represents your fret-hand fingers. Remember that your fret-hand fingers are numbered from one to four (index to pinky). To play this exercise, place your first finger on the 1st fret and pick the note. Next, place your second finger on the 2nd fret and strike this note. Place your third finger on the third fret and play this note. Finally, position your fourth finger on the fourth fret and pick this note. You are now ready to repeat this pattern starting on the second fret. The exercise 1-2-3-4, should be repeated on each fret until your fourth finger reaches the twelfth fret. You then play the exercise backwards (4-3-2-1) to the 1st fret. This exercise should be practiced on two or more strings every day.

Alternate Picking Exercise # 1

1234
Ascending

Continue up to the 12th fret

Descending

Continue down to the first fret

Alternate Picking Exercise # 2

1243
Ascending

Continue up to the 12th fret

Descending

Continue down to the first fret

Alternate Picking Exercise # 3

1324
Ascending

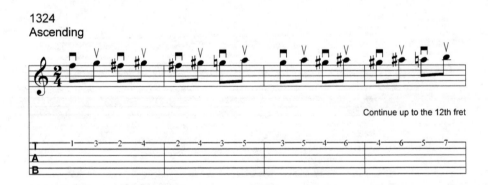

Continue up to the 12th fret

Descending

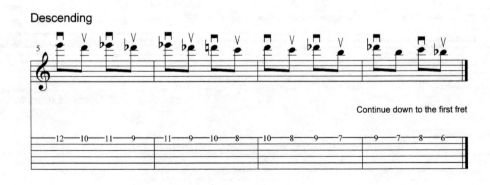

Continue down to the first fret

Alternate Picking Exercise # 4

1342
Ascending

Continue up to the 12th fret

Descending

Continue down to the first fret

Alternate Picking Exercise # 5

1423
Ascending

Continue up to the 12th fret

Descending

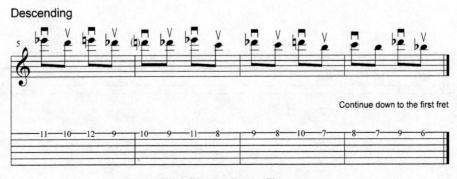

Continue down to the first fret

Alternate Picking Exercise # 6

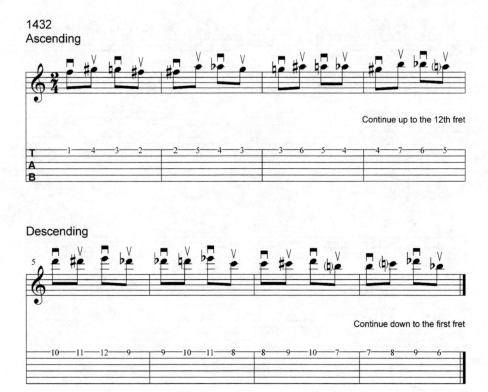

1432
Ascending

Continue up to the 12th fret

Descending

Continue down to the first fret

Alternate Picking Exercise # 7

C Major Scale Fingering 1

Scales are an excellent way to develop picking dexterity. The first note is played with a down-stroke and the second is played with an up-stroke. Continue this pattern with each successive note.

Alternate Picking Exercise # 8

C Major Scale Fingering 2

Here is a second way to play the C major scale.

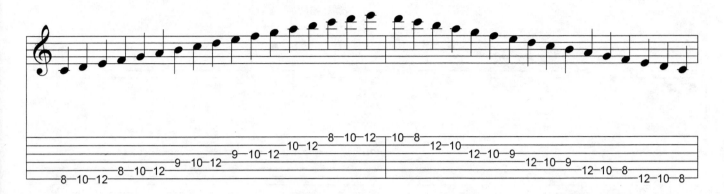

Alternate Picking Exercise # 9

A Minor Scale

Alternate Picking Exercise # 10

A Minor Pentatonic Scale

Alternate Picking Exercise # 11
C Pentatonic Major Scale

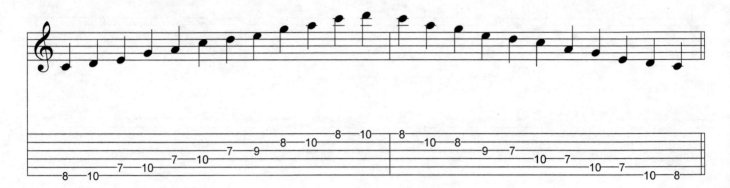

Alternate Picking Exercise # 12
A Harmonic Minor Scale

Alternate Picking Exercise # 13
C Major Scale in Thirds

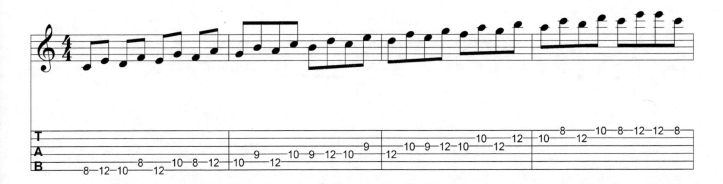

Alternate Picking Exercise # 14
A Minor Scale in Thirds

Alternate Picking Exercise # 15

A Harmonic Minor Scale in Thirds

Quick Tips for Faster Fingers

Pickin' It

Don J. MacLean

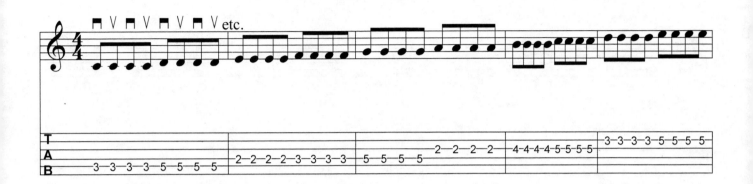

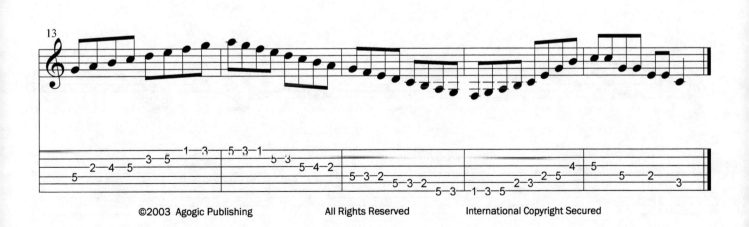

In the Hall of the
Mountain King

From Peer Gynt

E. Grieg
Arr. by Don J. MacLean

Quick Tips for Faster Fingers

Brandenburg Concerto
No. 5 in D Major
1st Movement Excerpt

J.S. Bach
Arr. by Don J. MacLean

Brandenburg Concerto No. 2
Excerpt

J. S. Bach
Arr. by Don J. MacLean

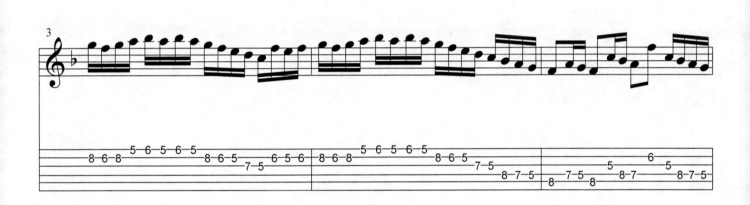

The *tr* symbol found in Brandenburg Concerto No. 2, is an abbreviation for the trill. A trill is an ornamental device that is produced by rapidly alternating between the **principal** note (the note directly under the *tr* symbol) and its upper auxiliary note. The **upper auxiliary** note, also known as an upper neighbour note, is a note that is either a whole tone or a semitone above the principal note. In this case, since the scale of the moment is F major, you will alternate between the notes F (upper auxiliary) and E (principal). The trill is usually performed by playing alternating pull-offs and hammer-ons. The number of repercussions (pull-offs and hammer-ons) is determined by the tempo of the music and by the virtuosity of the performer. Measure 8 is played as follows:

Symphony No. 26
Third Movement Excerpt

W. A. Mozart
Arr. by Don J. MacLean

Study No. 31

F. Wohlfahrt
Arr. by Don J. MacLean

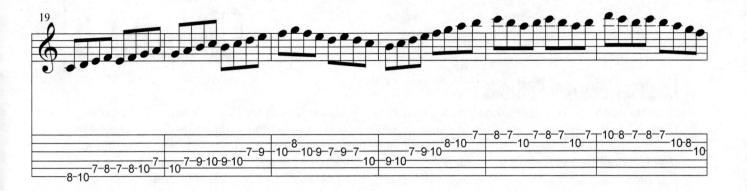

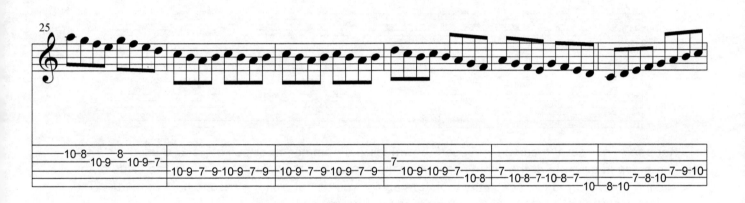

Chapter 5

Hammer-ons and Pull-offs

In some contexts, you want to play notes that sound fluid. The term for this is **legato**. The best way to play notes in a legato fashion is to use hammer-ons and/or pull-offs. A **hammer-on** is produced by striking the lower pitched note and then sounding the higher note with your fret-hand. You do not pick the note that is hammered. The **pull-off** is the opposite of the hammer-on. To perform a pull-off you pick the higher pitched note and then sound the lower note with your fret-hand. Place both fingers on the notes to be sounded and then pull-off the higher finger so that the lower note is heard. You do not pick the note that is pulled off.

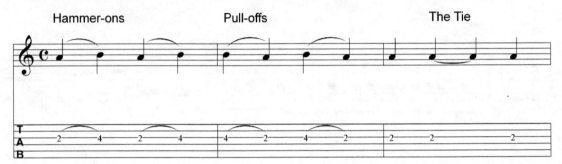

Keep in mind that the curved line used to symbolize a hammer-on or pull-off is also used for a tie. The notes in a tie are of the same pitch. A tie increases the time value of a note by the value of the second note. As you can see in the tablature above, you do not pick the second note of the tie. The first note of the tie is held for the duration of the two notes combined.

Hammer-on Pull-off Exercise # 1

Pick the first note on each string and hammer-on the rest. Play the descending version of the exercise by picking the first note on the string and sound the remaining notes with pull-offs.

Practice exercise 1 on each fret up to the 12th fret. Once you reach the twelfth fret play the entire exercise backwards to the first fret. This is a great endurance exercise—if your hands get fatigued, just play the exercise up to the 7th fret. Every week our so, make it your goal to add one or more additional frets. Hammer-on and pull-off exercises 1-5 should be performed on each fret and played to the 12th fret.

Hammer-on Pull-off Exercise # 2

1234
Ascending   Descending

Repeat this pattern commencing on each fret.

etc.

Hammer-on Pull-off Exercise # 3

Finger combo 1-2-3 and 2-3-4
In addition to playing this exercise with fingers 1-2-3, you should also play it using fingers 2-3-4.
Remember that you are only picking the first note on each string.

Hammer-on Pull-off Exercise # 4

Finger combo 1-2-4

Hammer-on Pull-off Exercise # 5

Finger combo 1-3-4

Quick Tips for Faster Fingers

Hammer-on Pull-off Exercise # 6

C Major

You should also practice scales with hammer-ons and pull-offs. Below you will find a fingering for the C major scale.

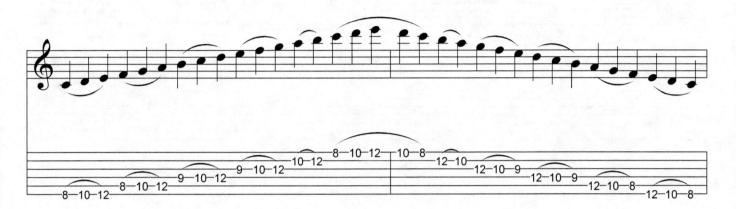

Hammer-on Pull-off Exercise # 7

A Minor

Hammer-on Pull-off Exercise # 8
A Minor Pentatonic

Quick Tips for Faster Fingers

Pullin' it Off

Don J. MacLean

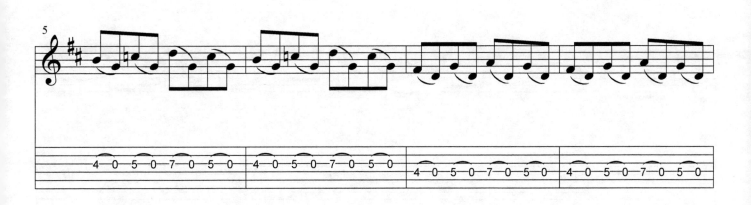

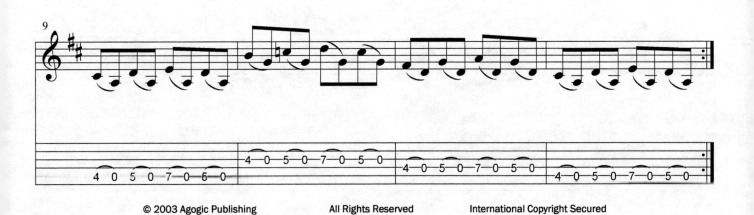

Study No. 46
Excerpt

F. Wohlfahrt
Arr. by Don J. MacLean

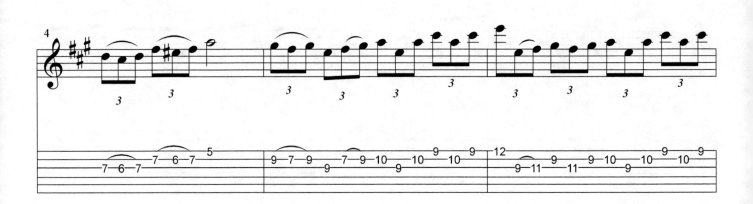

    Quick Tips for Faster Fingers

Study No. 45
Excerpt

F. Wohlfahrt
Arr. by Don J. MacLean

Study No. 11
Excerpt

R. Kreutzer
Arr. by Don J. MacLean

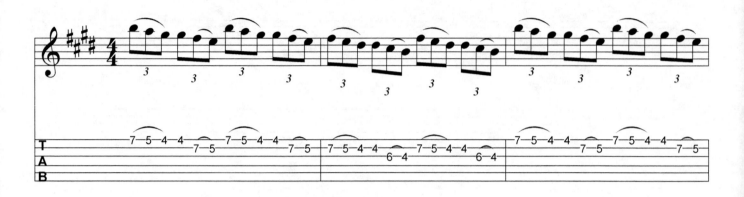

Quick Tips for Faster Fingers

Study No. 13
Excerpt

J. F. Mazas
Arr. by Don J. MacLean

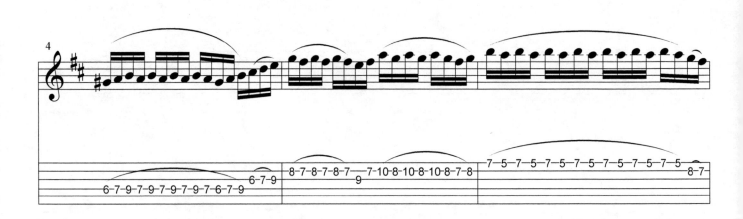

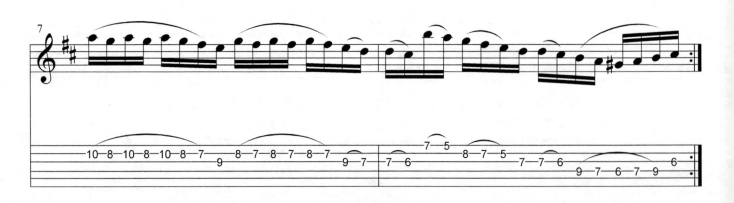

Chapter 6

Tapping Exercises

Tapping is a technique that will allow you to produce some very quick legato passages and play notes that would otherwise be an impossible stretch. Tapping requires you to use your pick-hand to hammer-on and/or pull-off notes on the fretboard. To do this, you hold your pick as you normally would, and use the middle finger of your pick-hand to hammer-on or pull-off the appropriate notes.

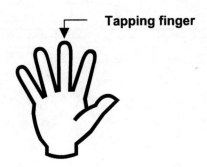

Tapping finger

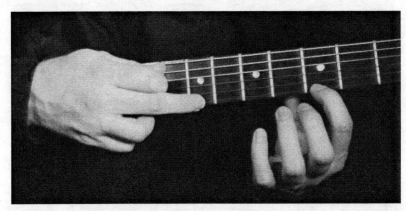

To perform tapping, hammer the middle finger of your picking hand onto the fretboard. Like normal hammer-ons your goal is to produce a clear note. Once this note is produced you then pull-off your finger to sound the note that is fretted with your left hand. The "T" is used to indicate a tapped note.

The above picture shows how to perform this example.

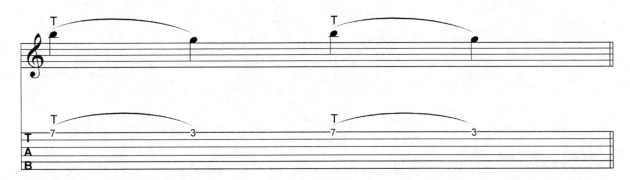

Tapping Exercise # 1

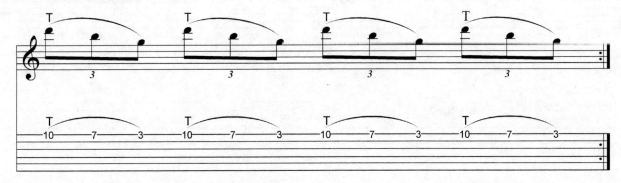

Quick Tips for Faster Fingers

45

Tapping Exercise # 2

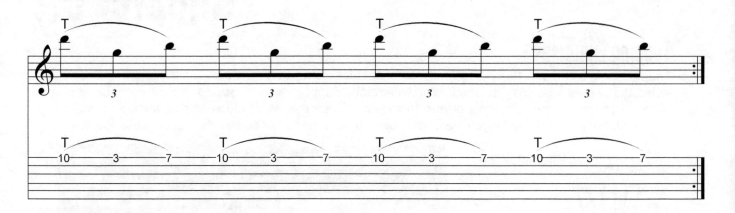

Tapping Exercise # 3

Tapping Exercise # 4

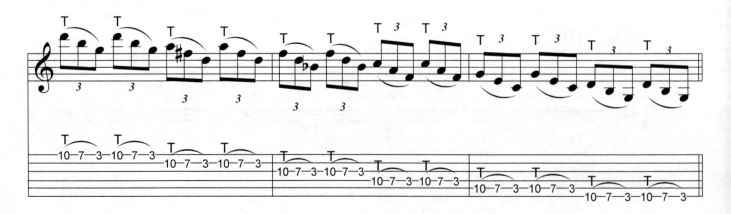

Quick Tips for Faster Fingers

Tapping Exercise # 5

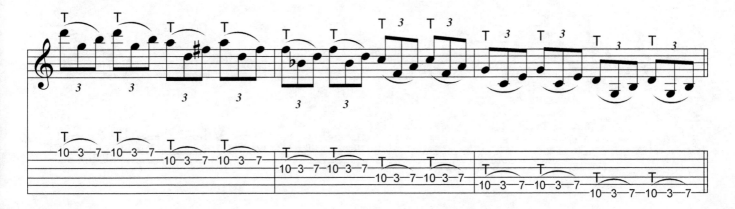

Tapping Exercise # 6

A Minor Scale

Tap This!

Don J. MacLean

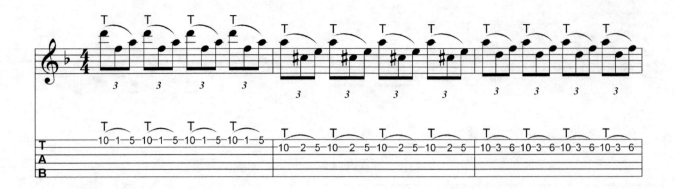

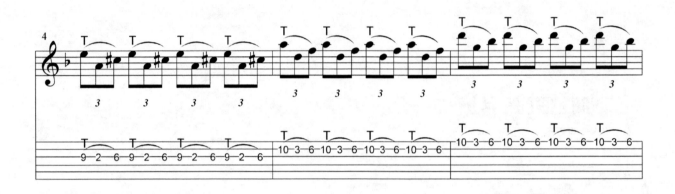

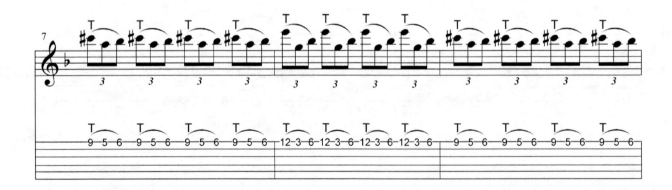

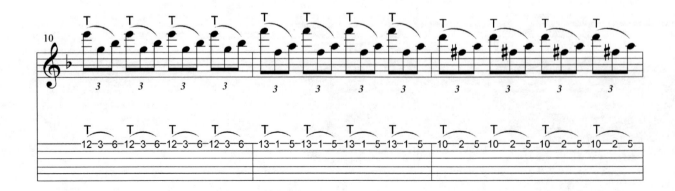

Quick Tips for Faster Fingers

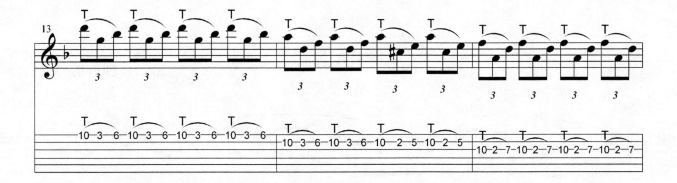

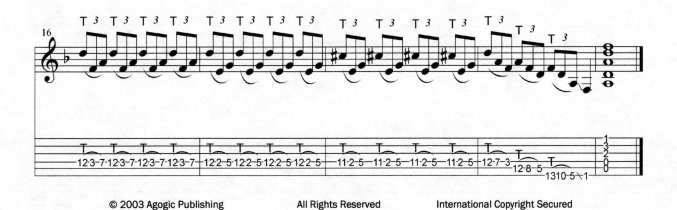

There are a few big stretches in this piece that may take some time to master. With practice you will find them easy to perform. The diagonal slash (\) found on beat four of the second last measure is used to indicate a slide. To perform this, tap the F on the 13th fret, pull-off to the D on the 10th fret, pull-off to the A on the 5th fret and then slide down to the F on the 1st fret.

Morning
From Peer Gynt

E.Grieg
Arr. by Don J. MacLean

Quick Tips for Faster Fingers

Chapter 7

Sweep Picking

Sweep picking is used primarily for arpeggios. An arpeggio is produced by playing the notes of a chord one-by-one. Arpeggios are often played with just one note per string. Instead of using alternate picking to play arpeggios, sweep picking is more efficient. In sweep picking, you use as many continuous down or up-strokes as possible. If the arpeggio changes direction, you then reverse your picking.

Here is how it works: In *Sweep Picking Exercise #1* you will see an E major arpeggio. In this fingering for the arpeggio, there is one note on each string. The way to play this is to use one continuous down-stroke for strings 5-1 and then one continuous up-stroke for strings 2-4. Sweep picking gets its name from the way it looks when performed—it looks like you are sweeping across the strings with your pick. In some arpeggios you will need to play two notes on a string. To do this, use alternate picking on the strings that have two notes and sweep pick the rest.

Sweep Picking Exercise # 1
E major arpeggio

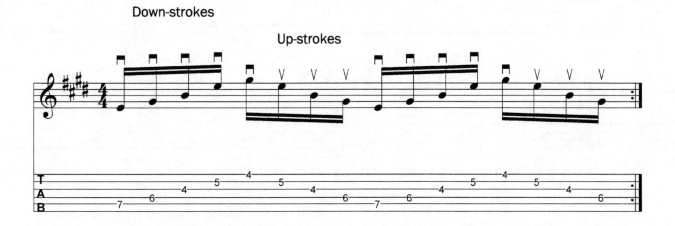

Sweep Picking Exercise # 2
E major arpeggio

Sweep Picking Exercise # 3
E minor arpeggio

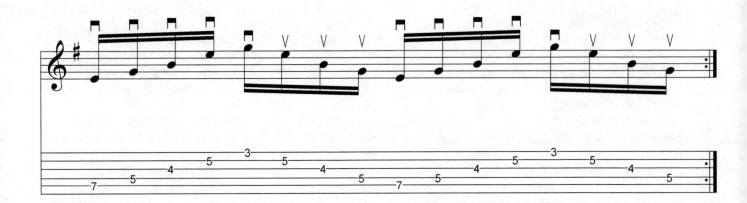

Sweep Picking Exercise # 4
E minor arpeggio

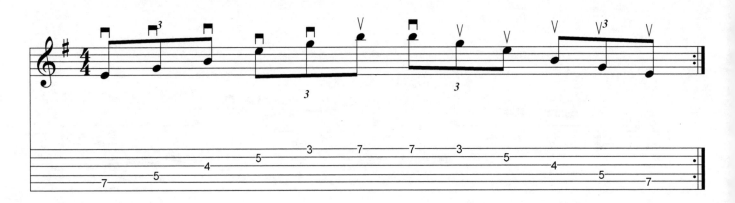

Sweep Picking Exercise # 5

Sweep Picking Exercise # 6

Once you reach measure 10, repeat the entire exercise starting on the second fret.

ascending

descending

Study No. 28
Excerpt

J. F. Mazas
Arr. by Don J. MacLean

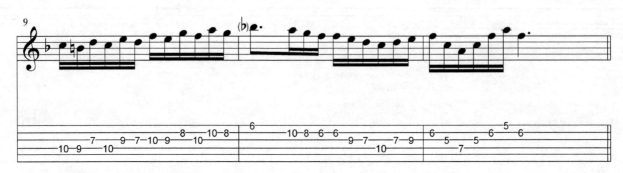

Quick Tips for Faster Fingers

Study No. 34
Excerpt

F. Wohlfahrt
Arr. by Don J. MacLean

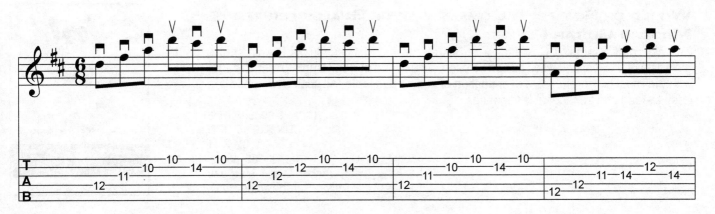

Available from

AGOGIC PUBLISHING

WORLD OF SCALES: A COMPENDIUM OF SCALES FOR THE MODERN GUITAR PLAYER

THE WORLD OF SCALES: A COMPENDIUM OF SCALES FOR THE MODERN GUITAR PLAYER shows guitarists of all levels how scales can be used. The World of Scales provides the reader with the most comprehensive examination of scales available. All scales are shown in easy-to-read and transposable fingerings.

ISBN 1-896595-07-3
$25.95 CDN $19.95 USD
8½ X 11
165 pages
Author: Don J. MacLean
Editor: Rob Bowman Ph.D.

WORLD OF SCALES: A COMPENDIUM OF SCALES FOR ALL INSTRUMENTS 2ND EDITION

THE WORLD OF SCALES: A COMPENDIUM OF SCALES FOR ALL INSTRUMENTS enables intermediate to advanced musicians to understand: how scales are built; how chords are constructed and interact with scales; and how to apply modalization to any scale. The World of Scales provides the reader with the most thorough examination of scales available. All scales are shown in treble and bass clefs.

ISBN 1-896595-21-9
$25.95 CDN $19.95 USD
8½ X 11
96 pages
Author: Don J. MacLean

QUICK TIPS FOR FASTER FINGERS

Wouldn't you rather play faster, more accurately and with better technique? Add a new dimension to your playing with 54 specially chosen and created technique builders for massive chops. Whether you are a beginner or intermediate player, you will refer to this text again and again.

ISBN 1-896595-10-3
$22.95 CDN $17.95 USD
8½ X 11
62 pages
Author: Don J. MacLean

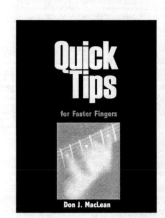

ABSOLUTE ESSENTIALS OF MUSIC THEORY

In this easy-to-follow self-study guide, you will learn the basics of: music notation, intervals, scales, chords, harmonized scales, and rhythm. Answer key included.

ISBN 1-896595-12-X
$22.95 CDN $17.95 USD
8½ X 11
68 pages
Author: Don J. MacLean

MUSIC ESSENTIALS: IMPROVISER

Laminated Reference Chart

MUSIC ESSENTIALS: IMPROVISER provides the intermediate musician with the tools to improvise over chords. Start with a scale and view the chords that can be used or, select a chord and view its scale options. All scales are shown in both treble and bass clefs. The Improviser is the first chart to provide musicians with easy access to this information.

ISBN 1-896595-23-5
$7.99 CDN $6.99 USD
1 Double sided page; 11 X 17
Blue and silver

GUITAR ESSENTIALS: IMPROVISER

Laminated Reference Chart

GUITAR ESSENTIALS: IMPROVISER provides the intermediate guitarist with the tools to improvise over chords. Start with a scale and view the chords that can be used or, select a chord and view its scale options. All scale forms are shown in transposable neck diagrams. The Improviser is the first chart to provide guitar players with easy access to this information.

ISBN 1-896595-19-7
$7.99 CDN $6.99 USD
1 Double sided page;11 X 17
Black and gold

GUITAR ESSENTIALS: CHORD MASTER

Laminated Reference Chart

GUITAR ESSENTIALS: THE CHORD MASTER shows guitarists of all levels how to quickly and easily play 1176 of the most common guitar chords.

ISBN 1-896595-13-8
$4.99 CDN $3.99 USD
1 Double sided page; 8½ X 11
Black and red

GUITAR ESSENTIALS: SCALE MASTER 1

Laminated Reference Chart

GUITAR ESSENTIALS: THE SCALE MASTER 1 shows you how to play the most common scales. Major, minor, harmonic minor, melodic minor, major pentatonic, minor pentatonic, blues and the composite blues scales are all included in this chart.

ISBN 1-896595-11-1
$4.99 CDN $3.99 USD
1 Double sided page; 8½ X 11
Black and red

ORDER FORM

Canadian residents, prices shown in Canadian funds.

Title	Price + GST	Shipping	Sub total	Qty.	Total
World of Scales: A Compendium of Scales for the Modern Guitar Player	$25.95+$2.17	$5.00	$33.12		
World of Scales: A Compendium of Scales for all Instruments	$25.95+$2.17	$5.00	$33.12		
Guitar Essentials: Chord Master	$4.99+$0.49	$2.00	$7.48		
Guitar Essentials: Scale Master 1	$4.99+$0.49	$2.00	$7.48		
Guitar Essentials: Improviser	$7.99+$0.70	$2.00	$10.69		
Music Essentials: Improviser	$7.99+$0.70	$2.00	$10.69		
Quick Tips for Faster Fingers	$22.95+$1.96	$4.00	$28.84		
Absolute Essentials of Music Theory	$22.95+$1.96	$4.00	$28.84		
			Grand total		

Discounts available on bulk orders. For information fax 604-540-4419

US residents, prices shown in US funds.

Title	Price	Shipping	Sub total	Qty.	Total
World of Scales: A Compendium of Scales for the Modern Guitar Player	$19.95	$6.00	$25.95		
World of Scales: A Compendium of Scales for all Instruments	$19.95	$6.00	$25.95		
Guitar Essentials: Chord Master	$3.99	$3.00	$6.99		
Guitar Essentials: Scale Master 1	$3.99	$3.00	$6.99		
Guitar Essentials: Improviser	$6.99	$3.00	$9.99		
Music Essentials: Improviser	$6.99	$3.00	$9.99		
Quick Tips for Faster Fingers	$17.95	$5.00	$22.95		
Absolute Essentials of Music Theory	$17.95	$5.00	$22.95		
			Grand total		

Discounts available on bulk orders. For information fax 1-604-540-4419

Ship To:

Name _____

Address _____

City/ Prov/State _____

Postal/Zip Code _____

Phone _____

Email _____

Mail this order form today with your money order payable to:

Agogic Publishing
406-109 Tenth Street
New Westminster, BC
V3M 3X7
Phone 604-290-2692
Fax 604-540-4419